The Real Book Multi-Tracks Vol. 3

For C, B♭, E♭ & Bass Clef Instruments

ALL BLUES

Play-Along

To access online content visit:
www.halleonard.com/mylibrary

Enter Code
8342-4283-6772-3629

ISBN 978-1-4950-7475-2

T0056095

HAL•LEONARD®
7777 W. Bluemound Rd. P.O. Box 13819 Milwaukee, WI 53213

For more information on the Real Book series, including community forums, please visit
www.OfficialRealBook.com

Visit Hal Leonard Online at
www.halleonard.com

Contents

All Blues

— MILES DAVIS

C VERSION

BACK AT THE CHICKEN SHACK

– Jimmy Smith

BILLIE'S BOUNCE
(BILL'S BOUNCE)

– CHARLIE PARKER

C VERSION

LAST X, TO ⊕

AFTER SOLOS, D.S. AL ⊕
(PLAY PICKUP) (TAKE REPEAT)

BIRK'S WORKS

- DIZZY GILLESPIE

C VERSION

FINE

AFTER SOLOS, D.S. AL FINE
(PLAY PICKUPS) (TAKE REPEAT)

BLUES BY FIVE

- RED GARLAND

C VERSION

SOLO B♭ BLUES (NO ANTICIPATIONS)
AFTER SOLOS, D.S. AL ⊕
(PLAY PICKUP) (NO REPEAT)

C-JAM BLUES

— DUKE ELLINGTON

MR. P.C.

— JOHN COLTRANE

ONE FOR DADDY-O

— NAT ADDERLEY

Reunion Blues

— MILT JACKSON

Turnaround

- Ornette Coleman

C Version

All Blues

14

MED. (BLUES)

- MILES DAVIS

B♭ Version

Back at the Chicken Shack

- Jimmy Smith

B♭ Version

BILLIE'S BOUNCE
(BILL'S BOUNCE)

— CHARLIE PARKER

B♭ VERSION

LAST X, TO ⊕

AFTER SOLOS, D.S. AL ⊕
(PLAY PICKUP) (TAKE REPEAT)

BIRK'S WORKS

- DIZZY GILLESPIE

FINE

AFTER SOLOS, D.S. AL FINE
(PLAY PICKUPS) (TAKE REPEAT)

BLUES BY FIVE

— RED GARLAND

SOLO C BLUES (NO ANTICIPATIONS)
AFTER SOLOS, D.S. AL ⊕
(PLAY PICKUP) (NO REPEAT)

C-Jam Blues

— Duke Ellington

MR. P.C.

— JOHN COLTRANE

ONE FOR DADDY-O

— NAT ADDERLEY

REUNION BLUES

— MILT JACKSON

Turnaround

— ORNETTE COLEMAN

All Blues

— Miles Davis

BILLIE'S BOUNCE
(BILL'S BOUNCE)

— CHARLIE PARKER

Eb VERSION

(FAST BLUES)

LAST X, TO ⊕

AFTER SOLOS, D.S. AL ⊕
(PLAY PICKUP) (TAKE REPEAT)

BIRK'S WORKS

– DIZZY GILLESPIE

Blues By Five

— Red Garland

SOLO G BLUES (NO ANTICIPATIONS)
AFTER SOLOS, D.S. AL ⊕
(PLAY PICKUP) (NO REPEAT)

C-Jam Blues

— Duke Ellington

MR. P.C.

– JOHN COLTRANE

SOLO ON A MINOR BLUES
AFTER SOLOS, D.C. AL ⊕
(TAKE REPEAT)

ONE FOR DADDY-O

— NAT ADDERLEY

Turnaround

— ORNETTE COLEMAN

LAST X, TO ⊕

⊕ A

AFTER SOLOS, D.S. AL ⊕
(PLAY PICKUP) (TAKE 2ⁿᵈ ENDING)

All Blues

— MILES DAVIS

C BASS VERSION

BILLIE'S BOUNCE
(BILL'S BOUNCE)

(FAST BLUES)

C BASS VERSION

— CHARLIE PARKER

AFTER SOLOS, D.S. AL ⊕
(PLAY PICKUP) (TAKE REPEAT)

Birk's Works

— Dizzy Gillespie

FINE

AFTER SOLOS, D.S. AL FINE
(PLAY PICKUPS) (TAKE REPEAT)

Blues By Five

— Red Garland

SOLO B♭ BLUES (NO ANTICIPATIONS)
AFTER SOLOS, D.S. AL ⊕
(PLAY PICKUP) (NO REPEAT)

MR. P.C.

— JOHN COLTRANE

C BASS VERSION

SOLO ON C MINOR BLUES
AFTER SOLOS, D.C. AL ⊕
(TAKE REPEAT)

ONE FOR DADDY-O

— NAT ADDERLEY

REUNION BLUES

— MILT JACKSON

Turnaround

— ORNETTE COLEMAN

LAST X, TO ⊕

AFTER SOLOS, D.S. AL ⊕
(PLAY PICKUP) (TAKE 2nd ENDING)

THE REAL BOOK MULTI-TRACKS

The interactive, online audio interface includes:

- tempo control
- looping
- buttons to turn each instrument on or off
- lead sheet with follow-along marker
- melody performed by a saxophone or trumpet on the "head in" and "head out."

The full stereo tracks can also be downloaded and played off-line. Separate lead sheets are included for C, B-flat, E-flat and Bass Clef instruments.

1. MAIDEN VOYAGE PLAY-ALONG

Autumn Leaves • Blue Bossa • Doxy • Footprints • Maiden Voyage • Now's the Time • On Green Dolphin Street • Satin Doll • Summertime • Tune Up.
00196616 Book with Online Media $17.99

2. MILES DAVIS PLAY-ALONG

Blue in Green • Boplicity (Be Bop Lives) • Four • Freddie Freeloader • Milestones • Nardis • Seven Steps to Heaven • So What • Solar • Walkin'.
00196798 Book with Online Media $17.99

3. ALL BLUES PLAY-ALONG

All Blues • Back at the Chicken Shack • Billie's Bounce (Bill's Bounce) • Birk's Works • Blues by Five • C-Jam Blues • Mr. P.C. • One for Daddy-O • Reunion Blues • Turnaround.
00196692 Book with Online Media $17.99

4. CHARLIE PARKER PLAY-ALONG

Anthropology • Blues for Alice • Confirmation • Donna Lee • K.C. Blues • Moose the Mooche • My Little Suede Shoes • Ornithology • Scrapple from the Apple • Yardbird Suite.
00196799 Book with Online Media $17.99

5. JAZZ FUNK PLAY-ALONG

Alligator Bogaloo • The Chicken • Cissy Strut • Cold Duck Time • Comin' Home Baby • Mercy, Mercy, Mercy • Put It Where You Want It • Sidewinder • Tom Cat • Watermelon Man.
00196728 Book with Online Media $17.99

HAL•LEONARD®
www.halleonard.com

Prices, content and availability subject to change without notice.

The Best-Selling Jazz Book of All Time Is Now Legal!

The Real Books are the most popular jazz books of all time. Since the 1970s, musicians have trusted these volumes to get them through every gig, night after night. The problem is that the books were illegally produced and distributed, without any regard to copyright law, or royalties paid to the composers who created these musical masterpieces.

Hal Leonard is very proud to present the first legitimate and legal editions of these books ever produced. You won't even notice the difference, other than all the notorious errors being fixed: the covers and typeface look the same, the song lists are nearly identical, and the price for our edition is even cheaper than the originals!

Every conscientious musician will appreciate that these books are now produced accurately and ethically, benefitting the songwriters that we owe for some of the greatest tunes of all time!

VOLUME 1
00240221	C Edition	$39.99
00240224	B♭ Edition	$39.99
00240225	E♭ Edition	$39.99
00240226	Bass Clef Edition	$39.99
00240292	C Edition 6 x 9	$35.00
00240339	B♭ Edition 6 x 9	$35.00
00147792	Bass Clef Edition 6 x 9	$35.00
00451087	C Edition on CD-ROM	$29.99
00240302	A-D CD Backing Tracks	$24.99
00240303	E-J CD Backing Tracks	$24.95
00240305	S-Z CD Backing Tracks	$24.99
00110604	Book/USB Flash Drive Backing Tracks Pack	$79.99
00110599	USB Flash Drive Only	$50.00

VOLUME 2
00240222	C Edition	$39.99
00240227	B♭ Edition	$39.99
00240228	E♭ Edition	$39.99
00240229	Bass Clef Edition	$39.99
00240293	C Edition 6 x 9	$35.00
00125900	B♭ Edition 6 x 9	$35.00
00451088	C Edition on CD-ROM	$30.99
00240351	A-D CD Backing Tracks	$24.99
00240352	E-I CD Backing Tracks	$24.99
00240353	J-R CD Backing Tracks	$24.99
00240354	S-Z CD Backing Tracks	$24.99

VOLUME 3
00240233	C Edition	$39.99
00240284	B♭ Edition	$39.99
00240285	E♭ Edition	$39.99
00240286	Bass Clef Edition	$39.99
00240338	C Edition 6 x 9	$35.00
00451089	C Edition on CD-ROM	$29.99

VOLUME 4
00240296	C Edition	$39.99
00103348	B♭ Edition	$39.99
00103349	E♭ Edition	$39.99
00103350	Bass Clef Edition	$39.99

VOLUME 5
00240349	C Edition	$39.99

VOLUME 6
00240534	C Edition	$39.99

Also available:
00240264	The Real Blues Book	$34.99
00310910	The Real Bluegrass Book	$29.99
00240440	The Trane Book	$22.99
00125426	The Real Country Book	$39.99
00240137	Miles Davis Real Book	$19.95
00240355	The Real Dixieland Book C Edition	$29.99
00122335	The Real Dixieland Book B♭ Edition	$29.99
00240235	The Duke Ellington Real Book	$19.99
00240268	The Real Jazz Solos Book	$30.00
00240348	The Real Latin Book C Edition	$37.50
00127107	The Real Latin Book B♭ Edition	$35.00
00240358	The Charlie Parker Real Book	$19.99
00240331	The Bud Powell Real Book	$19.99
00240437	The Real R&B Book	$39.99
00240313	The Real Rock Book	$35.00
00240323	The Real Rock Book – Vol. 2	$35.00
00240359	The Real Tab Book	$32.50
00240317	The Real Worship Book	$29.99

THE REAL CHRISTMAS BOOK
00240306	C Edition	$32.50
00240345	B♭ Edition	$32.50
00240346	E♭ Edition	$32.50
00240347	Bass Clef Edition	$32.50
00240431	A-G CD Backing Tracks	$24.99
00240432	H-M CD Backing Tracks	$24.99
00240433	N-Y CD Backing Tracks	$24.99

THE REAL VOCAL BOOK
00240230	Volume 1 High Voice	$35.00
00240307	Volume 1 Low Voice	$35.00
00240231	Volume 2 High Voice	$35.00
00240308	Volume 2 Low Voice	$35.00
00240391	Volume 3 High Voice	$35.00
00240392	Volume 3 Low Voice	$35.00
00118318	Volume 4 High Voice	$35.00
00118319	Volume 4 Low Voice	$35.00

THE REAL BOOK – STAFF PAPER
00240327		$10.99

HOW TO PLAY FROM A REAL BOOK
by Robert Rawlins
00312097		$17.50

THE REAL BOOK – ENHANCED CHORDS
arranged by David Hazeltine
00151290		$29.99

Complete song lists online at www.halleonard.com
Prices, content, and availability subject to change without notice.

HAL•LEONARD®
7777 W. BLUEMOUND RD. P.O. BOX 13819 MILWAUKEE, WI 53213

1116

Presenting the Hal Leonard JAZZ PLAY-ALONG® SERIES

For use with all B-flat, E-flat, Bass Clef and C instruments, the Jazz Play-Along® Series is the ultimate learning tool for all jazz musicians. With musician-friendly lead sheets, melody cues, and other split-track audio choices included, these first-of-a-kind packages help you master improvisation while playing some of the greatest tunes of all time. FOR STUDY, each tune includes a split track with: melody cue with proper style and inflection • professional rhythm tracks • choruses for soloing • removable bass part • removable piano part. FOR PERFORMANCE, each tune also has: an additional full stereo accompaniment track (no melody) • additional choruses for soloing.

87. **DIXIELAND**
00843111......................$16.99

90. **THELONIOUS MONK CLASSICS**
00841262......................$16.99

91. **THELONIOUS MONK FAVORITES**
00841263......................$16.99

92. **LEONARD BERNSTEIN**
00450134......................$16.99

93. **DISNEY FAVORITES**
00843142......................$16.99

94. **RAY**
00843143......................$16.99

95. **JAZZ AT THE LOUNGE**
00843144......................$16.99

96. **LATIN JAZZ STANDARDS**
00843145......................$16.99

97. **MAYBE I'M AMAZED***
00843148......................$16.99

98. **DAVE FRISHBERG**
00843149......................$16.99

99. **SWINGING STANDARDS**
00843150......................$16.99

100. **LOUIS ARMSTRONG**
00740423......................$16.99

101. **BUD POWELL**
00843152......................$16.99

102. **JAZZ POP**
00843153......................$16.99

103. **ON GREEN DOLPHIN STREET
& OTHER JAZZ CLASSICS**
00843154......................$16.99

104. **ELTON JOHN**
00843155......................$16.99

105. **SOULFUL JAZZ**
00843151......................$16.99

106. **SLO' JAZZ**
00843117......................$16.99

107. **MOTOWN CLASSICS**
00843116......................$16.99

108. **JAZZ WALTZ**
00843159......................$16.99

109. **OSCAR PETERSON**
00843160......................$16.99

110. **JUST STANDARDS**
00843161......................$16.99

111. **COOL CHRISTMAS**
00843162......................$16.99

112. **PAQUITO D'RIVERA – LATIN JAZZ***
48020662......................$16.99

113. **PAQUITO D'RIVERA – BRAZILIAN JAZZ***
48020663......................$19.99

114. **MODERN JAZZ QUARTET FAVORITES**
00843163......................$16.99

115. **THE SOUND OF MUSIC**
00843164......................$16.99

116. **JACO PASTORIUS**
00843165......................$16.99

117. **ANTONIO CARLOS JOBIM – MORE HITS**
00843166......................$16.99

118. **BIG JAZZ STANDARDS COLLECTION**
00843167......................$27.50

119. **JELLY ROLL MORTON**
00843168......................$16.99

120. **J.S. BACH**
00843169......................$16.99

121. **DJANGO REINHARDT**
00843170......................$16.99

122. **PAUL SIMON**
00843182......................$16.99

123. **BACHARACH & DAVID**
00843185......................$16.99

124. **JAZZ-ROCK HORN HITS**
00843186......................$16.99

125. **SAMMY NESTICO**
00843187......................$16.99

126. **COUNT BASIE CLASSICS**
00843157......................$16.99

127. **CHUCK MANGIONE**
00843188......................$16.99

128. **VOCAL STANDARDS (LOW VOICE)**
00843189......................$16.99

129. **VOCAL STANDARDS (HIGH VOICE)**
00843190......................$16.99

130. **VOCAL JAZZ (LOW VOICE)**
00843191......................$16.99

131. **VOCAL JAZZ (HIGH VOICE)**
00843192......................$16.99

132. **STAN GETZ ESSENTIALS**
00843193......................$16.99

133. **STAN GETZ FAVORITES**
00843194......................$16.99

134. **NURSERY RHYMES***
00843196......................$17.99

135. **JEFF BECK**
00843197......................$16.99

136. **NAT ADDERLEY**
00843198......................$16.99

137. **WES MONTGOMERY**
00843199......................$16.99

138. **FREDDIE HUBBARD**
00843200......................$16.99

139. **JULIAN "CANNONBALL" ADDERLEY**
00843201......................$16.99

140. **JOE ZAWINUL**
00843202......................$16.99

141. **BILL EVANS STANDARDS**
00843156......................$16.99

142. **CHARLIE PARKER GEMS**
00843222......................$16.99

143. **JUST THE BLUES**
00843223......................$16.99

144. **LEE MORGAN**
00843229......................$16.99

145. **COUNTRY STANDARDS**
00843230......................$16.99

146. **RAMSEY LEWIS**
00843231......................$16.99

147. **SAMBA**
00843232......................$16.99

148. **JOHN COLTRANE FAVORITES**
00843233......................$16.99

149. **JOHN COLTRANE – GIANT STEPS**
00843234......................$16.99

150. **JAZZ IMPROV BASICS**
00843195......................$19.99

151. **MODERN JAZZ QUARTET CLASSICS**
00843209......................$16.99

152. **J.J. JOHNSON**
00843210......................$16.99

154. **HENRY MANCINI**
00843213......................$16.99

155. **SMOOTH JAZZ CLASSICS**
00843215......................$16.99

156. **THELONIOUS MONK – EARLY GEMS**
00843216......................$16.99

157. **HYMNS**
00843217......................$16.99

158. **JAZZ COVERS ROCK**
00843219......................$16.99

159. **MOZART**
00843220......................$16.99

160. **GEORGE SHEARING**
14041531......................$16.99

161. **DAVE BRUBECK**
14041556......................$16.99

162. **BIG CHRISTMAS COLLECTION**
00843221......................$24.99

163. **JOHN COLTRANE STANDARDS**
00843235......................$16.99

164. **HERB ALPERT**
14041775......................$16.99

165. **GEORGE BENSON**
00843240......................$16.99

166. **ORNETTE COLEMAN**
00843241......................$16.99

167. **JOHNNY MANDEL**
00103642......................$16.99

168. **TADD DAMERON**
00103663......................$16.99

169. **BEST JAZZ STANDARDS**
00109249......................$19.99

170. **ULTIMATE JAZZ STANDARDS**
00109250......................$19.99

171. **RADIOHEAD**
00109305......................$16.99

172. **POP STANDARDS**
00111669......................$16.99

174. **TIN PAN ALLEY**
00119125......................$16.99

175. **TANGO**
00119836......................$16.99

176. **JOHNNY MERCER**
00119838......................$16.99

177. **THE II-V-I PROGRESSION**
00843239......................$19.99

178. **JAZZ/FUNK**
00121902......................$16.99

179. **MODAL JAZZ**
00122273......................$16.99

180. **MICHAEL JACKSON**
00122327......................$16.99

181. **BILLY JOEL**
00122329......................$16.99

182. **"RHAPSODY IN BLUE" & 7 OTHER
CLASSICAL-BASED JAZZ PIECES**
00116847......................$16.99

183. **SONDHEIM**
00126253......................$16.99

184. **JIMMY SMITH**
00126943......................$16.99

185. **JAZZ FUSION**
00127558......................$16.99

186. **JOE PASS**
00128391......................$16.99

187. **CHRISTMAS FAVORITES**
00128393......................$16.99

188. **PIAZZOLLA – 10 FAVORITE TUNES**
48023253......................$16.99

189. **JOHN LENNON**
00138678......................$16.99

*These do not include split tracks.

1116

Jazz Instruction & Improvisation

BOOKS FOR ALL INSTRUMENTS FROM HAL LEONARD

AN APPROACH TO JAZZ IMPROVISATION
by Dave Pozzi
Musicians Institute Press

Explore the styles of Charlie Parker, Sonny Rollins, Bud Powell and others with this comprehensive guide to jazz improvisation. Covers: scale choices • chord analysis • phrasing • melodies • harmonic progressions • more.

00695135 Book/CD Pack.......................................$17.95

THE ART OF MODULATING
FOR PIANISTS AND JAZZ MUSICIANS
by Carlos Salzedo &
Lucile Lawrence
Schirmer

The Art of Modulating is a treatise originally intended for the harp, but this edition has been edited for use by intermediate keyboardists and other musicians who have an understanding of basic music theory. In its pages you will find: table of intervals; modulation rules; modulation formulas; examples of modulation; extensions and cadences; ten fragments of dances; five characteristic pieces; and more.

50490581 ....$19.99

BUILDING A JAZZ VOCABULARY
By Mike Steinel

A valuable resource for learning the basics of jazz from Mike Steinel of the University of North Texas. It covers: the basics of jazz • how to build effective solos • a comprehensive practice routine • and a jazz vocabulary of the masters.

00849911 ....$19.95

THE CYCLE OF FIFTHS
by Emile and Laura De Cosmo

This essential instruction book provides more than 450 exercises, including hundreds of melodic and rhythmic ideas. The book is designed to help improvisors master the cycle of fifths, one of the primary progressions in music. Guaranteed to refine technique, enhance improvisational fluency, and improve sight-reading!

00311114 ....$16.99

THE DIATONIC CYCLE
by Emile and Laura De Cosmo
Renowned jazz educators Emile and Laura De Cosmo provide more than 300 exercises to help improvisors tackle one of music's most common progressions: the diatonic cycle. This book is guaranteed to refine technique, enhance improvisational fluency, and improve sight-reading!

00311115 ....$16.95

EAR TRAINING
by Keith Wyatt,
Carl Schroeder and Joe Elliott
Musicians Institute Press
Covers: basic pitch matching • singing major and minor scales • identifying intervals • transcribing melodies and rhythm • identifying chords and progressions • seventh chords and the blues • modal interchange, chromaticism, modulation • and more.

00695198 Book/Online Audio $24.99

EXERCISES AND ETUDES FOR THE JAZZ INSTRUMENTALIST
by J.J. Johnson
Designed as study material and playable by any instrument, these pieces run the gamut of the jazz experience, featuring common and uncommon time signatures and keys, and styles from ballads to funk. They are progressively graded so that both beginners and professionals will be challenged by the demands of this wonderful music.

00842018 Bass Clef Edition $17.99
00842042 Treble Clef Edition $16.95

JAZZOLOGY
THE ENCYCLOPEDIA OF JAZZ THEORY FOR ALL MUSICIANS
by Robert Rawlins and
Nor Eddine Bahha
This comprehensive resource covers a variety of jazz topics, for beginners and pros of any instrument. The book serves as an encyclopedia for reference, a thorough methodology for the student, and a workbook for the classroom.

00311167 ....$19.99

JAZZ THEORY RESOURCES
by Bert Ligon
Houston Publishing, Inc.
This is a jazz theory text in two volumes. **Volume 1 includes**: review of basic theory • rhythm in jazz performance • triadic generalization • diatonic harmonic progressions and analysis • substitutions and turnarounds • and more.
Volume 2 includes: modes and modal frameworks • quartal harmony • extended tertian structures and triadic superimposition • pentatonic applications • coloring "outside" the lines and beyond • and more.

00030458 Volume 1 ....$39.95
00030459 Volume 2 ....$29.95

JOY OF IMPROV
by Dave Frank
and John Amaral
This book/audio course on improvisation for all instruments and all styles will help players develop monster musical skills! Book One imparts a solid basis in technique, rhythm, chord theory, ear training and improv concepts. **Book Two** explores more advanced chord voicings, chord arranging techniques and more challenging blues and melodic lines. The audio can be used as a listening and play-along tool.

00220005 Book 1 – Book/CD Pack.......................$27.99
00220006 Book 2 – Book/Online Audio...............$26.99

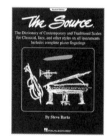

THE PATH TO JAZZ IMPROVISATION
by Emile and Laura De Cosmo
This fascinating jazz instruction book offers an innovative, scholarly approach to the art of improvisation. It includes in-depth analysis and lessons about: cycle of fifths • diatonic cycle • overtone series • pentatonic scale • harmonic and melodic minor scale • polytonal order of keys • blues and bebop scales • modes • and more.

00310904 ....$14.99

THE SOURCE
THE DICTIONARY OF CONTEMPORARY AND TRADITIONAL SCALES
by Steve Barta
This book serves as an informative guide for people who are looking for good, solid information regarding scales, chords, and how they work together. It provides right and left hand fingerings for scales, chords, and complete inversions. Includes over 20 different scales, each written in all 12 keys.

00240885 ....$19.99

21 BEBOP EXERCISES
by Steve Rawlins
This book/CD pack is both a warm-up collection and a manual for bebop phrasing. Its tasty and sophisticated exercises will help you develop your proficiency with jazz interpretation. It concentrates on practice in all twelve keys – moving higher by half-step – to help develop dexterity and range. The companion CD includes all of the exercises in 12 keys.

00315341 Book/CD Pack.......................................$17.95

HAL•LEONARD®
7777 W. BLUEMOUND RD. P.O. BOX 13819 MILWAUKEE, WI 53213

Visit Hal Leonard online at
www.halleonard.com

Prices, contents & availability subject to change without notice.

SNARE DRUM SOLOS Unaccompanied

MARIMBA/XYLOPHONE SOLOS with Piano Accompaniment

DRUM ENSEMBLES *Instrumentation as marked*

U.S. $7.99

RUBANK®

HAL•LEONARD®
7777 W. BLUEMOUND RD. P.O. BOX 13819 MILWAUKEE, WI 53213

ISBN-13: 978-1-4950-1477-2

Distributed By

HAL LEONARD

HL04479368

04479368

Hungarian Dance No.5

R-means Right Hand
L-means Left Hand

Hungarian Dance No.5

Marimba
or Xylophone

JOH. BRAHMS
Arr. by John B. Quick
Xylophonist

Copyright MCMXXXV by Rubank Inc., Chicago, Ill.
International Copyright Secured